Train Like Bayern Munich.
Play Like Bayern Munich.

15+ Training Exercises Used By Pep Guardiola That Will Have Your Team Playing Like FC Bayern Munich.

By Marcus DiBernardo

Introduction

This book is not designed to break down FC Bayern Munich's exact formations or movement patterns. It is not an in depth tactical analysis of each players roles and responsibilities in the Bayern system. If you are interested in details of specific systems you can pick up my book "Playing The Modern 4-2-3-1", "Playing The Modern 4-4-2 Diamond" or "Strategize". The focus of this book is to provide you with training ground exercises that focus on the major principles and concepts that FC Bayern Munich embrace in their style of play. These exercises are the same ones used at Bayern Munich under Pep Guardiola. Each exercise directly relates to the "Training Model" that fits with the Bayern "Game Model". Many of the exercises focus on the four phases of the game: attacking transition, attacking organization, defensive transition and defensive organization. There are also some passing patterns and functional dynamic finishing exercises. Playing the like Bayern requires excellent technical players, a belief in a passing system, tactical intelligence and the ability to break down teams and finish in the attacking third. Playing against Bayern can be very difficult because the majority of possession is usually with Bayern.

The 15+ exercises in this book will have your team training like FC Bayern Munich and after time playing like FC Bayern (training model = game model). I would strongly recommend that you also read my book "Tactical Periodization: Made Simple" in order to get a greater understanding of how to organize and create a training system like the one Guardiola uses. I hope you find the exercises rewarding! As always feel free to email me with any questions or comments

coachdibernardo@gmail.com

Table of Contents

Dynamic Running, Passing & Finishing
Bayern Munich

Grid: Attacking 1/3

Players: 10-12 field players, 2 keepers & 4 coaches

Instructions & Key Points:

This exercise is excellent for explosive running, dribbling and finishing. The player starts with agility by doing a figure "8" weaving between the 3 hurdles. Then (#1) the player sprints to first mannequin as the coach tosses him a ball to head back over the mannequin (#2), the player then back peddles to the red sticks laying on ground and bounds through them explosively, (#3) the player receives the ball from the next coach and dribbles quickly through the 2 tall yellow vertical sticks, (#4) player plays 1-2 combination with blue player and gets ball back to finish with a shot around the mannequins. The blue player behind the mannequin chooses what side to pop out of, so the player with the ball will have to read this and go to the opposite side to shoot. The player who just shot will take the players spot behind the mannequin as the mannequin passing player goes to join the line at the start of the drill.

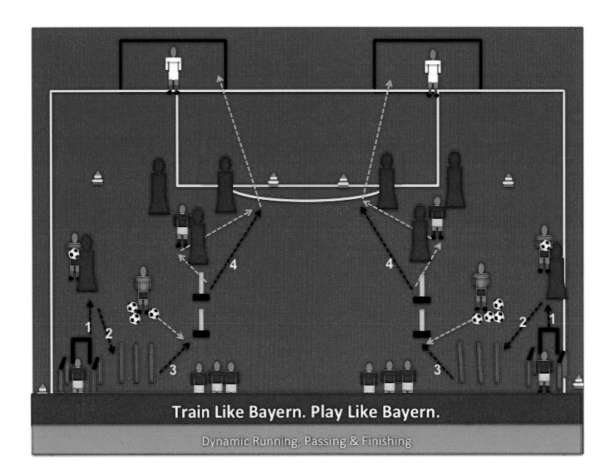

Train Like Bayern. Play Like Bayern.

Dynamic Running, Passing & Finishing

Dynamic Technical & 3v2 Finishing
Bayern Munich

Grid: Attacking 1/3

Players: 16 field players, 3 keepers & 2 coaches

Instructions & Key Points:

This training is a very effective way to work finishing using three different stations. The outside stations combine dynamic running, passing, dribbling and shooting. I would encourage you to create your own dynamic stations during the season in order to continuously challenge the players. These stations are the ones Bayern Munich were using. The middle of the field is used as a 3v2 to goal with another attacking and defending group ready to come on – rotating every other repetition. I recommend 10 minutes at each station for a total of 30 minutes.

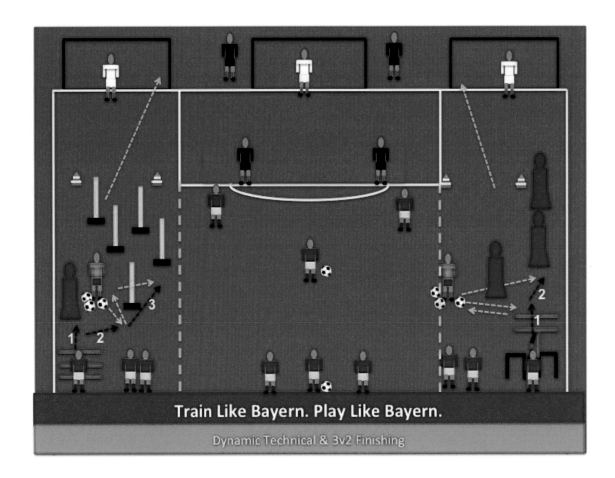

Train Like Bayern. Play Like Bayern.

Dynamic Technical & 3v2 Finishing

Compact Possession
Bayern Munich

Grid: 50x45 yards

Players: 18 field players (3 teams of 6) & 2 keepers

Instructions & Key Points:

This training game reflects the style or game model of Bayern Munich perfectly. The field is dived in half with one major condition. The team in possession must stay in the opponents half and use the halfway line as their line of restraint or line where their team pushes up to. They will not drop behind the half line when in possession. In this example you can see the red team is pressed into the blue teams half, while they are in possession. If the blue team wins the ball the red team is not allowed to drop. The red team must stay in the blue teams half and try to win the ball. If the blue team can break the press they will try to score on the red. Using this condition/rule assures possession is always in a very tight area. Players must think and play extremely quick to handle the pressure they are put under. When the ball is given away the group must transition quickly and pressure the ball to win it back. This training exercise is a miniature version of the Bayern game plan on match days. It also involves are four phases of the game – attacking transition, defending transition, attacking organization, defensive

organization.

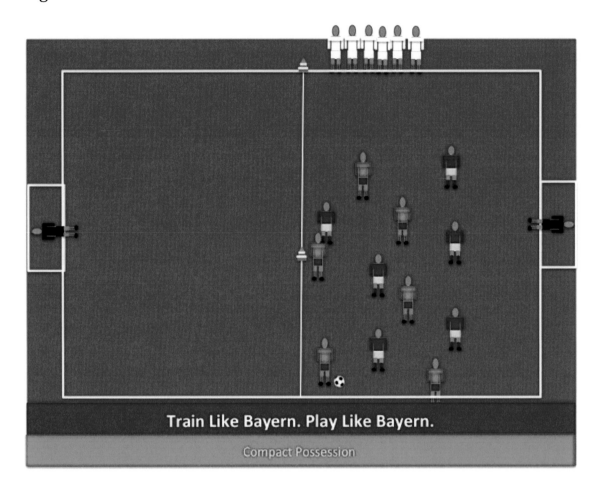

Passing Pattern + Dynamic Running Exercises
Bayern Munich

Grid: 25x25 yards

Players: 5-6 players

Instructions & Key Points:

This is a typical Bayern passing pattern that involves explosive movements, speed, bounding and passing. The passes are numbered in white and the stations are numbered in black. Each player will rotate one station forward for each repetition that is completed of the exercise. Station #1 - the player performs 2 passes, jumps over the hurdle, shuffles through the stick and mannequin and proceeds to station #2. Station #2- the player plays 2 passes and sprints to station #3. Station #3 the player performs 1 pass, bounds over sticks, steps quickly through speed rings and goes to station #4. Station #4 – the player dribbles at speed through the vertical sticks and gives the ball to player at station #1. If you want to speed the drill up have a few balls ready to go at station #1 and start play before the player on station #4 finishes.

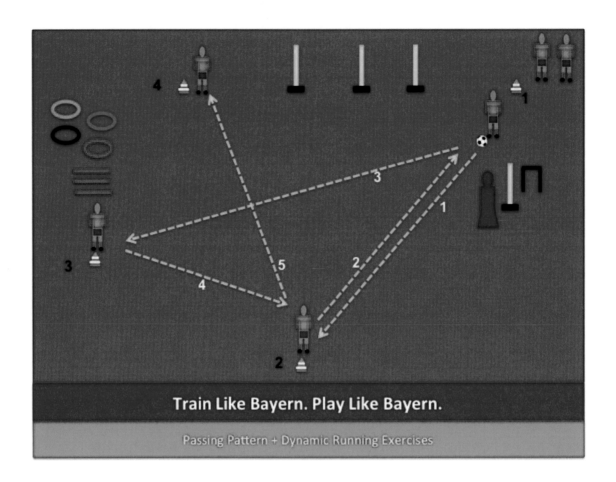

Train Like Bayern. Play Like Bayern.

Passing Pattern + Dynamic Running Exercises

Grid: 30x20 yards

Players: 9 - 12 field players (can adjust to 4v4v4)

Instructions & Key Points:

This is a straight-forward possession game that emphasizes defensive transition as soon as the ball is lost. The game starts with red and blue keep the ball together in possession (6v3). If a red player loses possession the white and blue team will possess the ball together as red transitions into defending/winning the ball back immediately. 2-touch maximum. The game can also be played 4v4v4 – adjust the size of the grid. Be sure to teach the four moments of the game,

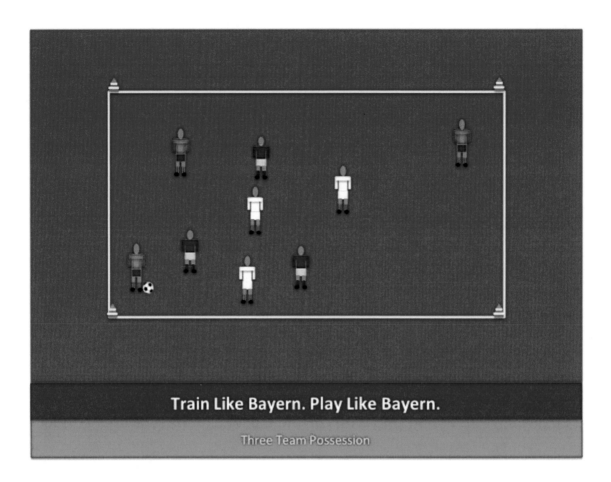

Train Like Bayern. Play Like Bayern.

Three Team Possession

7v2 Rondo
Bayern Munich

Grid: 10x10 yard grid

Players: 9 players

Instructions & Key Points:

Rondo is a keep away game that Barcelona has made famous. There are many variations of rondo that can be played. Bayern seem to use 7v2 more often than other rondos. The players in the middle try to win the ball as the outside players pass the ball to one another. The ultimate goal is to hit penetrating passes through the two defenders. If an outside player has his pass intercepted - he will switch with a middle player. The more skillful the player the less touches that are required. Start with a 2-touch restriction and reduce it to 1-touch if the players do well with 2-touch. For a complete breakdown of rondo check out my book "The Science of Rondo" on amazon.com

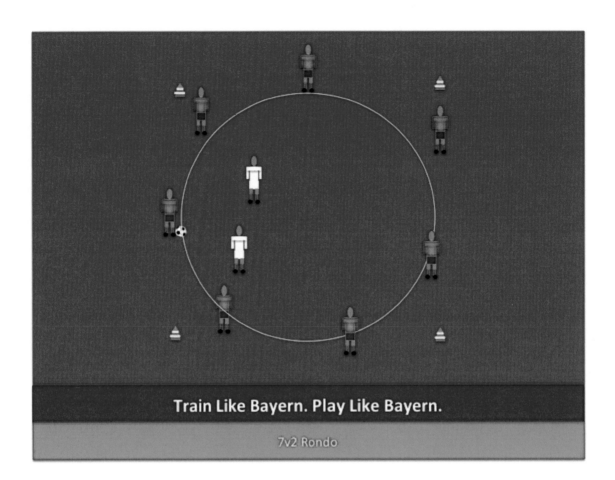

Train Like Bayern. Play Like Bayern.

7v2 Rondo

Passing Pattern
Bayern Munich

Grid: 25x20 yards

Players: 5-6 Players

Instructions & Key Points:

This diamond-passing pattern is one Bayern use that fits their style of

possession soccer. The ball is hit with pace to the receiving players

proper foot. The passes should be played 1st time if possible. Players

simply rotate counter-clockwise with each repetition. Focus on

accuracy, weight of the pass and overall passing rhythm of the exercise.

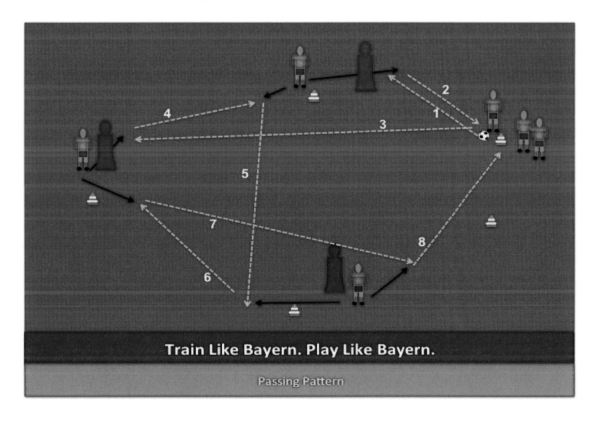

Train Like Bayern. Play Like Bayern.

Passing Pattern

Bayern Munich

Grid: Top of penalty box to top of penalty box – full width of field.

Players: 17 field players & 2 keepers

Instructions & Key Points:

This 9v9+1 training is played like a real game. The neutral player is always on the team in possession. Often the neutral for Bayern will be Ribery. He will play as an attacking player and is allowed to score for the team in possession of the ball. This 9v9+1 training is carried out for 30-45 minutes at a very high intensity rate. If the team have a match scheduled for a Sunday, this type of training would be done on Thursday (game minus 3 days). Guardiola follows the principles of tactical periodization, which dictate what types of trainings are done on what days. For detailed information on "Tactical Periodization" check out my book "Tactical Periodization: Made Simple" on amazon.com

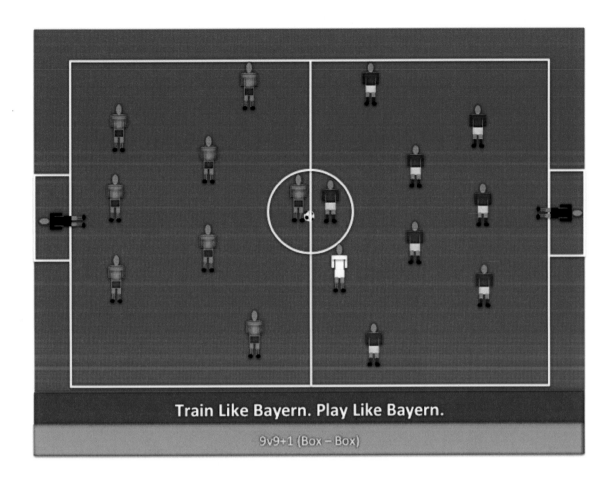

Train Like Bayern. Play Like Bayern.

9v9+1 (Box – Box)

Grid: Top of penalty box to top of penalty box – full width of field.

Players: 16 field players & 2 keepers

Instructions & Key Points:

This is the same as exercise #8 but without the neutral player. The four

phases of the game are always emphasized in these types of trainings.

Attacking transition, offensive organization, defensive transition and

defensive organization. Bayern make it a major point that the "training

model = game model".

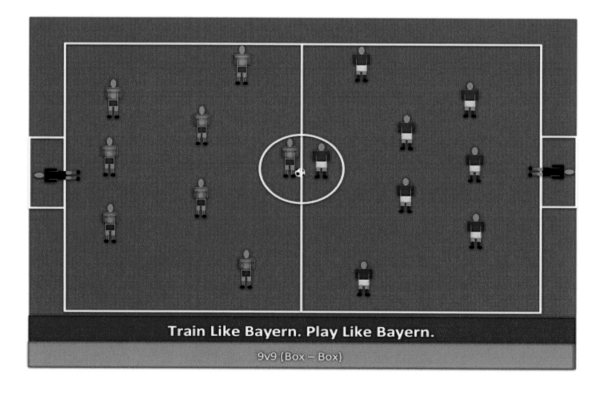

Train Like Bayern. Play Like Bayern.

9v9 (Box – Box)

6v6+1
Bayern Munich

Grid: Box-half field with width of penalty box as sidelines

Players: 13 field players & 2 keepers

Instructions & Key Points:

This is a smaller version of the 9v9+1 training using a smaller grid. The neutral player acts as an attacker for both teams and is allowed to score. The principles and goals of the training are the same. The four phases of the game are always emphasized and the intensity level is high. The workload and rest to work ratio will be less than the 9v9+1 training day. This type of training would most likely be on a Wednesday if the match is Sunday (game minus 4). Guardiola is very conscious of workload, duration and intensity levels in training. The idea is for the team to hit a stabilization of top performance week after week. By using the concepts of tactical periodization in training the hope is to stabilize performance at a very high level over the 10-month season. To the outside person the training may look like just a 6v6+1 to goal, but it is much more than that. This training like all the others is a piece of the bigger training puzzle that's fits into a very well organized tactical periodization weekly, monthly and season plan.

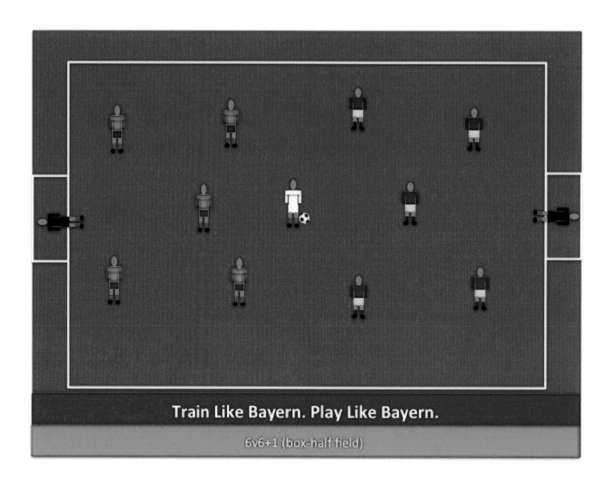

Train Like Bayern. Play Like Bayern.

6v6+1 (box-half field)

6v6 (box-half-field)
Bayern Munich

Grid: Box to half field with width of penalty box as sidelines

Players: 12 field players & 2 keepers

Instructions & Key Points:

This is the same exercise with the same key points and principles as

exercise #10 minus the neutral player!

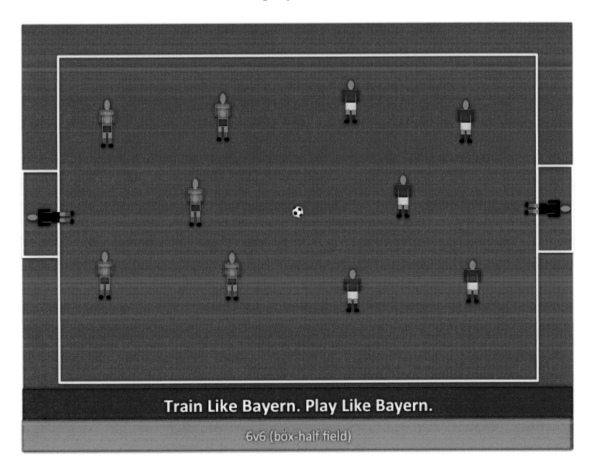

Train Like Bayern. Play Like Bayern.

6v6 (box-half field)

Bucket Skill Drill
Bayern Munich

Grid: 20x20 grid with barrel in middle

Players: 5-7 players

Instructions & Key Points:

This is a fun game that Bayern use in a few different ways. In this example the players flick the ball up and try to kick the ball in the air into the bucket. If the player misses another outside player will attempt to 1st time pass the ball into the bucket – if the ball is not bouncing they can flick it up and then kick it into the bucket. **Variation:** once ball is played into the bucket the entire group sprints 40 yards down field and back – they continue this pattern of scoring in the bucket and running until the desired distance is covered.

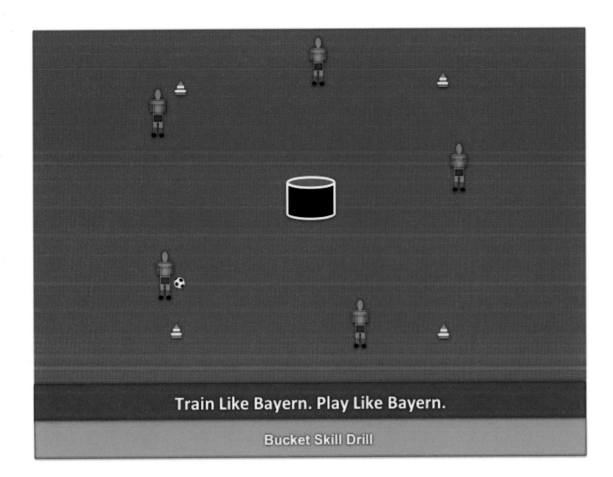

Train Like Bayern. Play Like Bayern.

Bucket Skill Drill

Grid: Attacking 1/3

Players: 5-7 players

Instructions & Key Points:

The first player starts on the side of the field behind the three low hurdles. The player will do a quick figure "8" shuffle through the three hurdles, bound through the red sticks on the ground, sprint to the first mannequin, turn and do 1-2 combination pass with player at the orange cone, receive the pass and dribble through the last two mannequins and shoot. After shooting the player will sprint to the orange cone where the player who played the 1-2 combination pass is located. The player will stay at the "pass station" until he gives one pass and then he will rotate back to the start at the hurdles to go again. This exercise like all the others should be done at speed and maximum intensity.

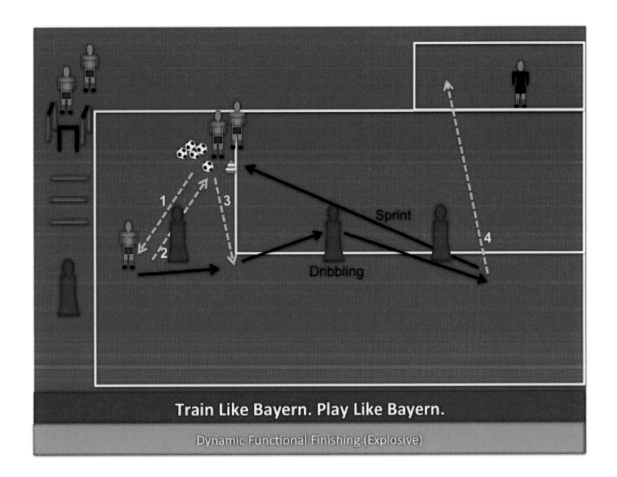

Train Like Bayern. Play Like Bayern.

Dynamic Functional Finishing (Explosive)

Grid: 20x15 grid

Players: 12 players

Instructions & Key Points:

This game is a variation of classic rondo, it demands extremely quick ball circulation to be successful. If players are not thinking fast and playing fast, possession will be lost. The game has 4 defenders in the middle (all one team – in this example the red team). The black team and the blue team will try and keep the ball away from the red team. Two blue players are placed inside the grid and all the rest of the blue and black team are placed outside the grid. A maximum of 2-touches is allowed. There are two ways to run this exercise: **First:** the red team will defend for 120 seconds straight. If they win the ball it goes back to the blue and black team. **Second:** if red wins the ball the inside two blue players need to work hard to win it back. If they are having difficulty winning the ball back – make the red team play 1-touch only when the win the ball. This exercise encompasses the Bayern game model.

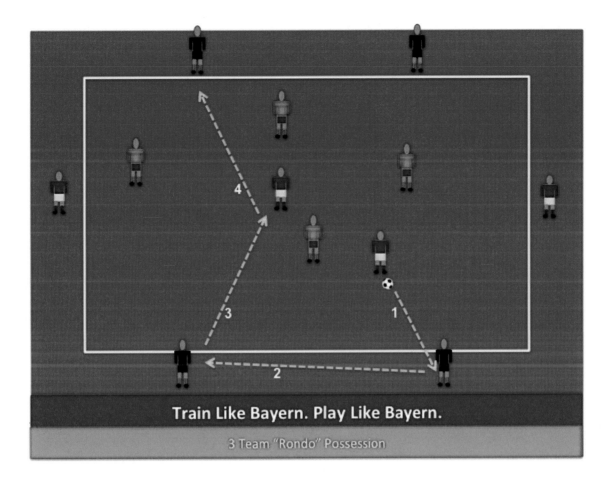

Train Like Bayern. Play Like Bayern.

3 Team "Rondo" Possession

Grid: 7x7 yard grid

Players: 5 Players

Instructions & Key Points:

This 4v1 (1-touch) is challenging and fast. Players will need to perform at a high level in order to keep the ball 1-touch in a 7x7 grid. Outside players should never find themselves in the corner of the grid. Outside players should move but never to far from the center because it destroys passing angles. If players are struggling with 1-touch go to 2-touch and than back to 1-touch. This 4v1 is yet another exercise that works on keeping the ball comfortably in tight situations. Bayern require players to be very good in possession, so this exercise fits their game model.

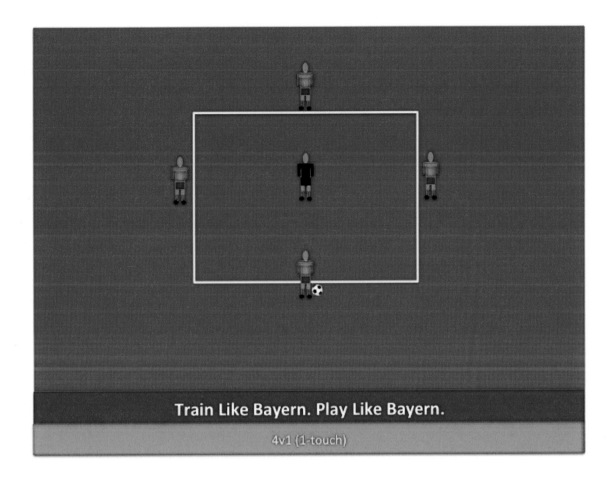

Train Like Bayern. Play Like Bayern.

4v1 (1-touch)

Three Goal Dynamic Functional Finishing
Bayern Munich

Grid: ¾ of the field with goal on sideline

Players: 15-18 field players & 3-6 keepers

Instructions & Key Points:

This is a very typical Bayern Munich training emphasizing finishing along with dynamic movements at full speed and high intensity. The idea is the most important aspect of this exercise. Each station is slightly different but they all involve dynamic full intensity running, passing, dribbling and shooting. This is yet another type of training that fits right into Guardiola's tactical periodization model. The rest to work ration is high but the intensity level is 100% when players are working. Finishing exercises are done frequently at Bayern. The game is often decided by the quality of finishing, so it makes perfect sense that Bayern work on finishing daily.

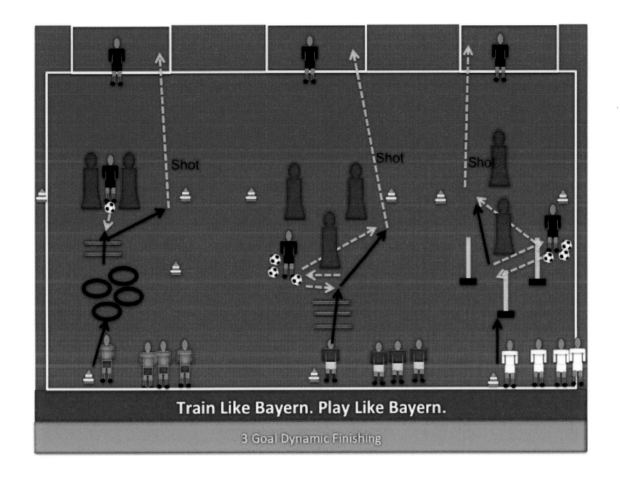

Train Like Bayern. Play Like Bayern.

3 Goal Dynamic Finishing

28025314R00021

Made in the USA
San Bernardino, CA
18 December 2015